Strengthening the Gates of Your Ministry

Apostle X. D. Madison, Sr.

Rhema Publishing Company

P.O. Box 35171

Las Vegas, Nevada 89133

ISBN: 1541152816
ISBN-13: 978-1541152816

DEDICATION

This book is dedicated to the five-fold ministry leaders around the world. May you find the guidance needed to man the gates of your ministry properly and with the right people.

ACKNOWLEDGEMENTS

I want to take this opportunity to thank my wife for life of 17 years, Lady Schantia Madison. Without your unwavering support, encouragement, understanding and prayers, this book could not have been written. God made you to be the woman that I needed in my corner and I honor you for who you are to me and our family. You continue to push me toward greatness! I love you for life.

I want to thank all my spiritual sons and daughters and the My Father's House Church family for your love and support. You all make leadership easy and I count it a privilege to have been afforded the opportunity to lead you all. Thank you to all my VOTIMA U.S.A and East Africa family for your support as we network and covenant together to take the message of Jesus Christ to the nations.

I want to give special thanks to my publishers as well as spiritual son and daughter, Pastors Baron and Tanya Angelique Samuel. You guys put in the work to ensure that this book reaches the masses.

Book Review

In these last days, more than ever there is an unprecedented attack on churches and ministries. We must raise the bar as it relates to spiritual warfare and discernment in this hour to ensure the gospel of the kingdom is not tainted. Fortifying the gates of one's ministry is of extreme importance. The Bible conveys to us in Matthew 13:25, "but while men slept the enemy came and sowed tares among the wheat and went his way." In this last hour that gatekeepers must rise and take their rightful place to protect the house of God from the influence of false teachings and false prophets, who would try to secretly infiltrate the church to lie in wait to deceive. Gatekeepers must be positioned at the gates of our ministries, disallowing diabolical sanctions of the enemy to stop the advancement of the Church.

God's servant, Apostle Xavier D. Madison, Sr. is a much sought after Apostolic voice that God has brought from obscurity in this decade to bring relevant truth to the Body of Christ. He is a preacher and teacher to leaders, and one of God's end time Generals. God is using him to empower sons and daughters around the world to restore the fear of the Lord within the church.

His Servant,

Prophetess Sheron Turner-McDuffie

CONTENTS

Foreword

Apostle Xavier D. Madison, Sr. delivers a cry to leaders to protect the ministry by electing and equipping gatekeepers. In the Bible, there were many gates referenced. Per Webster's Dictionary, a gate is an opening to an enclosure through a fence, wall etc. The word crasher was also used in this definition. It described how the gate can be violated as it is the entrance of an uninvited person or thing, which brings me to the importance of the gatekeeper.

In this hour, I believe that it is vital to watch what you are allowing into your eye gates, ear gates as well as the gates of your soul. Leaders be mindful of who you have as your gatekeepers in your personal lives and your ministries. My personal belief is all believers are gatekeepers, but there are some who have been called and anointed to this office. Some gatekeepers have been called to the local church while others internationally. Know your place.

My question to you is; have you secured your gates (soul, ministry, church and hearts)? Check your latches (gatekeepers) on your gates as they may have not been secured properly.

In the natural we must make sure the latches on the gates are secured so what we want to keep in or out of our gates will either stay in or stay out. All truth is parallel. The same applies in the spirit. You don't want anything that will wreak havoc to enter your soul, spirit, ministry.

Secure your gates because leaving them unsecured can be very dangerous and detrimental. Gatekeepers, what or who are you allowing access into your gates?

Mary Snell Ellison

INTRODUCTION

Strengthening the gates of your ministry is a book that was given to me, Apostle Xavier D. Madison, Sr. by divine revelation a few years ago. The Holy Spirit spoke to my heart after an extensive period of studying and personal observation regarding the spiritual and physical assaults that are coming against churches and ministries in this day and time. Many of these churches are called to be a beacon light in a dark and perishing world. The scripture declares in Matthew 11:12, from the days of John the Baptist until now, *the kingdom of heaven suffers violence and the violent taketh it by force.*

As an Apostle, I have seen firsthand how the devil attacks churches, causing confusion within the community of the saints. This book will serve as a guide to all leaders who have the responsibility of overseeing a church or ministry and those leaders who oversee areas of ministry within the church. If there has ever been a time when the church had need of spirit filled and committed men and women of God to arise and guard the gates of their church or ministry, that time is *now*.

I pray that this book will speak to the very core of your spirit; educate and empower you if you are a leader in any capacity in the house of God. Whether you know it or not, you are a gatekeeper and it's time for you to spring into action and guard the gates of your church/ministry.

CHAPTER 1
WHAT IS A GATEKEEPER?

What is a gatekeeper? The definition of gatekeeper is simply one who keeps a gate and controls the access into a place. The Bible speaks often about gatekeepers. These were people that were set apart and given the responsibility in the temple of the Lord to protect it from any opposing forces that would try and enter and wreak havoc in the camp of Israel. For example, 1 Chronicles 9:17-22, speaks of the gatekeepers who were responsible for the gates for the camps of the children of Levi. They were set in place to ensure that no danger or doom would be brought into the gates of the house of the Lord, the house of the tabernacle by assignment thus affecting the worship unto God in the temple. As we know the tribe of Levi represents the Levitical priesthood and they were a set apart people unto God that had the responsibility of serving and working in the temple. The primary target of the enemy is always the one who carries the word of God for the people- the Pastor or any other title that one has who bears the responsibility of overseeing the flock!

I was speaking with one of my colleagues in ministry a few weeks ago who pastors a vibrant young church in Southern Georgia. He proceeded to tell me how one night at his mid-week service a warlock walked into the church and began to release demonic incantations. As the man sat and uttered words from his mouth, my Pastor friend said that suddenly he felt numbness in his right arm and his stomach began to hurt like he had never experienced in his life. He immediately stops teaching and began to call the church to rebuke the demonic assignment that this possessed man attempted to release against him.

The power of God which resides within the name and blood of Jesus Christ defeats the powers of darkness every time. This is just an example of how important gatekeepers are in the ministry. The intercessory gatekeepers must position themselves in the sanctuary so that they can pray and watch out for any demonic activity that occurs in the house of the Lord. The gatekeepers in the church of today have very similar and important roles and responsibilities in this hour. We are presently hearing about how many church and ministry visions are being attacked spiritually and naturally throughout the Body of Christ.

I'm reminded of an incident that occurred a few years ago, in the Southern part of the United States. Sadly, the devil launched a deadly assault against a local church. Satan influenced a young man to walk into a church one night during mid-week service. He sat quietly near among the members and leaders of the church. After a while, the demon spirit that was influencing and operating within him led the young man to draw a weapon and shoot. His actions left many innocent people dead, including the Pastor of the church. Many debate if this was avoidable, but I believe that gatekeepers play such an important role in the house of the Lord. There will be times a gatekeeper may need to aggressively confront evil in those that seek to do the church harm. It's imperative that we understand that in the Old Testament the children of God dealt primarily with natural forces that opposed the people of God and tried to enter the camp.

In today's church, we deal with both the natural and the spiritual forces. Although we do understand that the scripture says in Ephesians 6: 12, that we wrestle not against flesh and blood, but against principalities, against powers, against the rulers of the darkness of this age, against spiritual hosts of wickedness in the heavenly places. However, we must also understand that flesh and blood can come into our settings under the influence of all types of evil spirits and we must confront them physically if physical force is warranted. The escalation of demonic activity is at an all-time high in this hour that we live, and things will get worse as the end of days and the rapture of the church nears. The scripture says that "in the latter day's perilous times would come" (2 Timothy 3:1) and we are truly living in those days that the Apostle Paul admonished us concerning. Therefore, I believe that we must be vigilant at strengthening the gates of our churches and making sure that the right gatekeepers are consecrated, set apart and anointed to keep the gates of the house of the Lord.

As the founder, Apostle and senior Overseer of My Father's House Church, I always stress to my leadership team and servant staff about how important it is for them to guard their gates and stay watchful for both spiritual and natural forces that could possibly seek to do the church harm. These attacks occur from within and without and we must always be on guard and watchful. Satan is the author of confusion and it is his desire to cause confusion, disharmony and dissension within the community of the saints, thus hindering the momentum of the church/ministry.

CHAPTER 2
WHAT ARE THE GATES OF YOUR CHURCH

Many believe when you speak about gatekeepers it is solely referencing the role of intercessors as they are charged to remain on the wall; but I want to introduce some revelation that the Lord has shared with me to share with the body of Christ. When I refer to gates, as I previously stated in the last chapter these are access points into your ministry or church where people serve and are actively involved in carrying out the vision of the church. I consider every ministry in your church as a gate. From the intake ministry to the parking lot ministry and all those in between, they each represent a point of access and the operators or those who oversee those areas are referred to in this book as the *gatekeepers*.

Many years ago, the Lord begin to reveal to me a divine strategy on how to train and release others to help me to oversee the house of God and the vision that he had entrusted to me. As an Apostle in the Lord's church, I truly believe that to grow and expand our ministry reach we must have the right people in key positions and strategically placed in the church as gatekeepers. When this operation lacks, the church is exposed to diverse attacks.

In the latter chapters, I will speak on the qualifications and role of a gatekeeper. We must make sure that the gatekeeper is not only qualified but are passionate about serving in an assigned area. The divine strategy that the

Lord had me to implement was found in the Old

Testament in the book of Exodus Chapter 18:13- 23,

13 And it came to pass on the morrow, that Moses sat to judge the people: and the people stood by Moses from the morning unto the evening.
14 And when Moses' father in law saw all that he did to the people, he said, What is this thing that thou doest to the people? why sittest thou thyself alone, and all the people stand by thee from morning unto even?
15 And Moses said unto his father in law, Because the people come unto me to enquire of God:
16 When they have a matter, they come unto me; and I judge between one and another, and I do make them know the statutes of God, and his laws.
17 And Moses' father in law said unto him, The thing that thou doest is not good.
18 Thou wilt surely wear away, both thou, and this people that is with thee: for this thing is too heavy for thee; thou art not able to perform it thyself alone.
19 Hearken now unto my voice, I will give thee counsel, and God shall be with thee: Be thou for the people to God-ward, that thou mayest bring the causes unto God:
20 And thou shalt teach them ordinances and laws, and shalt shew them the way wherein they must walk, and the work that they must do.
21 Moreover thou shalt provide out of all the people able men, such as fear God, men of truth, hating covetousness; and place such over them, to be rulers of thousands, and rulers of hundreds, rulers of fifties, and rulers of tens:
22 And let them judge the people at all seasons: and it shall be, that every great matter they shall bring unto thee, but every small matter they shall judge: so shall it be easier for thyself, and they shall bear the burden with thee.
23 If thou shalt do this thing, and God command thee so, then thou shalt be able to endure, and all this people shall also go to their place in peace.

Moses was charged with judging the people daily from sunrise to sunset and this wasn't a good thing that he was doing. I believe that it's never the will of God that our church or ministries be a one man or woman show. For this reason, many men and women of God who Pastor have died prematurely, are frustrated in ministry and some deal with all types and forms of bodily sicknesses such as stress, high blood pressure, worry and anxiety. Unfortunately, many of them are contemplating leaving the ministry because the load of ministry seemingly is unbearable.

I am reminded of my journey during my early years of pastoral ministry and how I attempted to do everything and be everything to everyone and the ministry. I found myself at a place of frustration and burnout very quickly-

boy do I thank God that I'm no longer a Pastor, but an Apostle and those pastoral responsibilities has been relegated to my staff ministers and elders. The ministry burnout, frustrations and sicknesses are most of the time because of leaders carrying the entire load of ministry on their shoulders; and trying to guard every gate. Preventing things from entering the ministry that would cause problems and addressing every problem that arises from within the ministry is not the sole role of the Pastor or leadership.

God allowed Moses' father-in-law, Jethro, to speak into his life giving him a strategy to lighten his load of ministry tremendously. Those people that Moses was charged to select and set apart are what I refer to as gatekeepers. To a certain degree, these gatekeepers have shared responsibility in overseeing what God had entrusted to Moses' care. I want to pause and speak wisdom into the life of every leader/gatekeeper. Whenever your senior leader selects and sets you apart, you have been divinely deleted by God and have a responsibility to help and assist your leader with overseeing all that God has entrusted to them. You become accountable to God and your leader.

Most of our churches have many ministries that we offer such as (children's ministry, praise ministry, deacons ministry, women's ministry, intercessory ministry, men's ministry etc.). These ministries represent gates of access that the enemy can come through if they are not manned properly by gatekeepers, which are overseers of these areas of ministry. However, the devil is always trying to find ways to come inside our local churches to stir up problems from within the gates and wreak havoc and his only access is through the gates.

Over 20 years ago, I worked in the petrochemical industry at a local chemical plant and each day that I came to work we had to acquire access into the plant by showing our identification badge. If we did not properly identify ourselves, we were not allowed access through the security gate. I remember a few times coming to work without my identification badge and even though the security gatekeeper recognized my face and knew who I was, he still could not allow me access.

At first, I did not understand this because I felt he should have allowed me access since he knew who I was; yet I began to see it from another perspective as the Spirit of the Lord gave revelation. The gatekeeper was responsible for doing his job and not compromising the security plan, policies, procedures and protocols that were in place by his superiors. One compromise would open the door to another, and the Bible declares in Song of

Solomon 2:15 “that the little foxes spoils the vine”. What I did not understand at that time was that the gatekeeper understood the magnitude of his responsibility, the lives that were depending on him to protect that gate. An act of compromise by allowing the wrong person in could have created a catastrophe; especially considering that we live in a society where terroristic activity has become the norm. Like the security officer, as a gatekeeper in your church or area of ministry, we must take our gates that serious.

The families and unity that you share within the community of the saints are worthy to be protected, both naturally and spiritually. All the devil wants to do is gain a foothold *(Ephesians 4:27)* so that he can cause chaos and confusion in the church. Therefore, we need gatekeepers who know how to keep a gate on post and watchful always.

Let me give a quick example so that you will understand the magnitude of what I'm saying. Let's say for instance, Sister Love is over the youth ministry which is flowing and doing well with no issues to speak of in that area. Later, Brother Discord decides that he wants to join because he was once a youth pastor at his last church. Brother Discord begins to express his interest to all the servants that are in the youth department that he's going to join the youth ministry team and make things better because the youth should be doing more in his opinion. He deliberately does not share this with the youth overseer Sister Love, but he shares it with her staff and her staff tells her about it because they recognize that Bro. Discord has some impure motives that are manifesting.

As the gatekeeper over this area of ministry, Sister Love is responsible for addressing this if Brother Discord approaches her about joining the area of ministry that she oversees. She would be within her scope of delegated authority and as a gatekeeper of that area to address this situation, because obviously, Brother Discord is under the influence of a bad spirit and is just waiting to seize a moment to get into the youth department and cause confusion and dissension among the ranks. Sister Love refuses to let him join this area of ministry because she sees how this brother's spirit would undermine her authority and run rampant in her area of ministry.

I want to interject some wisdom that I think would be very helpful to Pastors that have given their leaders/gatekeepers delegated authority to oversee areas of the ministry. It's important that you give the gatekeepers the latitude to address matters that arise at or within their gate if they are flowing in the same spirit that the senior leader is flowing in. Gatekeepers are there to help us as leaders and we must always support and endorse them when wise decisions are made that are in the best interest of the ministry.

Sadly, this situation could have been avoided had Brother Discord understood order, how to flow in ministry, followed protocol and took his ideas and concerns to the overseer of the youth department before speaking to others that serve within the youth department under the authority of Sister Love. Therefore, as pastors; we must educate and train potential gatekeepers before placing them in positions. They must first learn the spirit and protocols of the house. Oftentimes, people come into our churches/ministries after having been a part of several other churches and leaders who have different leadership styles and established protocols. Not every church is the same and not every leader is the same. Therefore, it's imperative that when people come into our church and express interest in serving in an area of ministry, they must first be required to learn the order and protocols of the house before being released to serve. At the church that I oversee, all new members who join our church family are required to complete New Member indoctrination training before being released to serve within the ministry. Additionally, those who desire to serve in higher levels of leadership are required to enroll in our Ministry preparatory school. This school teaches and prepares the members how to serve in ministry. In the upcoming chapters, I'm going address gatekeepers' role as whistle blowers in the ministry. Those leaders in the youth ministry did what they were trained to do and that was to advise the gatekeeper, Sis. Love regarding what Bro. Discord was contemplating doing and spreading throughout that area of ministry. In fact, the Word admonishes gatekeepers to be whistle blowers in Ezekiel 33:6.

> *But if the watchman see the sword come, and blow not the trumpet, and the people be not warned; if the sword come, and take any person from among them, he is taken away in his iniquity; but his blood will I require at the watchman's hand.*

If the gatekeeper, Sis. Love was not a strong gatekeeper and willing to confront the issues that were presented then it was only a matter of time before confusion would require the Pastors attention and he would have to deal with that which should have and could have been dealt with by the gatekeeper. I want to add that gatekeepers need to handle matters at the gate or within the gate and not let some things escalate and require the attention of the Pastor. Moses chose able-bodied men to lighten his load. If the pastor still must handle the issues that occur at or within a gate, then what good is the gatekeeper that's on the gate? Of course, certain matters should be brought to the pastor's attention, but the gatekeeper should handle things within their delegated scope of authority. Delegated authority, simply means that they are the ones who secures the gate so that nothing enters their area of ministry that would cause harm or hurt, thus affecting the church or stealing the Pastors time away from prayer and studying of the word.

I want to encourage every man or woman of God who have been given authority over an area of ministry to know that you are a gatekeeper and that your leader is depending on you to keep the gate so that confusion can be kept at a minimum in the house of God. By doing this you become one with him in carrying the load of ministry as a gatekeeper. So, gatekeepers, it's time for you to arise and get on your gates and make sure that you watch over and keep the gate of the ministry that has been delegated to you. As I prepare to close this chapter, I want us to look at the gatekeepers' ministry layout as written in the book

22 All these which were chosen to be porters in the gates were two hundred and twelve. These were reckoned by their genealogy in their villages, whom David and Samuel the seer did ordain in their set office.

23 So they and their children had the oversight of the gates of the house of the Lord, namely, the house of the tabernacle, by wards.

24 In four quarters were the porters, toward the east, west, north, and south.

25 And their brethren, which were in their villages, were to come after seven days from time to time with them.

26 For these Levites, the four chief porters, were in their set office, and were over the chambers and treasuries of the house of God.

27 And they lodged round about the house of God, because the charge was upon them, and the opening thereof every morning pertained to them.

28 And certain of them had the charge of the ministering vessels, that they should bring them in and out by tale.

29 Some of them also were appointed to oversee the vessels, and all the instruments of the sanctuary, and the fine flour, and the wine, and the oil, and the frankincense, and the spices.

of 1 Chronicles chapter 9:22-29

As I conduct verse by verse exposition of this scripture, I want to point out a few things. In verse 22 it reads they were chosen as gatekeepers and the seer had appointed them to that trusted office. Two points I want to make, the first one is that gatekeepers were chosen, hand selected by the prophet of God, the seer Samuel just as they are chosen inside our local churches by the men and women of God. I would venture to say that these gatekeepers were no ordinary men but exceptional men who were capable and honorable to be selected as gatekeepers. Please understand that gatekeeping is not gender restrictive. God uses both men and women to fulfill the functions and responsibilities of a gatekeeper.

Secondly, note that this was a trusted office. Being a gatekeeper is not just a position, but it is an office that's held in the church and a very important office at that. Verse 23- they and their children were put in charge and all had an assignment given to them and were responsible for the gates in the tabernacle and house of the Lord. When I read this verse, something leaped in my spirit because the responsibilities as gatekeepers are upon the children as well. This suggests to us that families should be actively involved in the house of God and working together to ensure that the house of God is kept free of confusion, dissension or anything that could hurt or hinder the vision.

When I think about children being engaged in ministry with their parents, I cannot help but to think about my youngest daughter Alexia, she's 16 years old and Lady Madison and I raised her up in the church from birth. She has grown to become a young leader in the vision at My Father's House Church and I would classify her as a young gatekeeper in training. There have been many times over the years that she has alerted me and my wife concerning issues and problems that she saw in the ministry and had they not been addressed it could have resulted into something major occurring in the ministry.

In verse 24- gatekeepers were assigned to different directions which suggests to us that every direction of the ministry must be covered and gatekeepers on duty. The devil is very crafty, and he desires to get into our ministries/churches in any way that he can or strike up confusion from within. Gatekeepers you are responsible for covering and guarding the church/ministry from the four corners- north, south, east and west. Therefore, if all gatekeepers are on watch then they will be able to sound the alarm whenever the spiritual forces attempt to come against the church and hinder the vision.

Verse 25- suggests to us that there were those men and women of God who were in training as gatekeepers in training who would from time to time learn the inner workings of the gatekeepers. Being an Apostle, I strongly urge Pastors to always have young leaders being groomed, trained and equipped to step up into areas of ministry because sometimes gatekeepers go bad!! In the upcoming chapters I will deal with this subject of "gatekeeper gone bad."

Before I conclude, I want to look at verse 26 and discuss the trusted office of the gatekeepers, there were four chief gatekeepers and they were Levites. This conveys to us that ministers, elders or staff pastors you are supposed to be chief gatekeepers in the church. The chief gatekeepers are those who exercise general oversight over the other gatekeepers ensuring that the ministry vision is protected, carried out in accordance to the heart of the senior leader's vision. They are supposed to be loyal to the senior leader first and foremost then to those in the church/ministry. They are Levites and should always walk in such a way that they remain set apart never becoming too common with those they serve and lead. Consider how the CEO of a company is typically not found dining in the company break room. While forging relationships with those leading you or that you serve is encouraged it must not be mistaken as being familiar (common) with them. This is very important, because oftentimes in the church chief gatekeepers become too common with subordinates and the level of respect is compromised and the vision suffers most of the time because familiarity will always breed contempt.

As a Levite/minister of the gospel, your allegiance should always be to God first and then to the senior leader that put you in place to help him oversee the house of

God. You have an important responsibility to oversee and you must be completely trustworthy.

In verse 27, they had the entire house of God covered all around because they had the responsibility of complete oversight as chief gatekeepers. This also suggests to us that sometimes; chief gatekeepers will know things and be told things that the senior leader might not know of but because you're a chief gatekeeper you are responsible for never withholding any information from the senior leader about or pertaining the house of God. I want to take a moment to share a real-life ministry experience as I attempt to help gatekeepers and Pastors. I'll never forget how many years ago, that there was sin in the camp (church) and it was among some of my leaders. Some of those who were not involved in the acts of sin but had full knowledge of what was going on were gatekeepers. Because of their allegiance to persons and personalities, friends etc.... they withheld the information from me because of their allegiance toward friendships and not purpose. The Lord will always expose sin when His servant is a praying man or woman and desire to lead the house of the Lord in righteousness and holiness. Gatekeepers you must settle it in your heart that your allegiance must always be to God and to your leader not to your friends, bosom buddies or those who you may engage in carnal relationships with. This is ministry, not reality television show!!!! In the upcoming chapter, I will deal with the informant aspect of the gatekeeper.

CHAPTER 3
QUALIFICATIONS OF A GATEKEEPER

I would venture to say that every Pastor or senior overseer of an assembly or local church have heard people tell you that they have your heart and are there for you, right? They will even go as far as saying that they have your back and will do all that they can to protect the ministry. Have you ever had people tell you that and then a short time later they are nowhere to be found, gone from the ministry/church etc.? Or what about the one we leaders hear most commonly "Pastor.... I feel my season is up" after only being there in the ministry for a few weeks or maybe months. This is common within the church these days, because faithful and committed hearted people are hard to find and as leaders we must never cease to pray as the scripture suggests to "pray to the God of the harvest that he would send laborers" (Matthew 9:38). I wrote this chapter so I could express my heart and to share briefly regarding what the qualifications of a gatekeeper are.

In the church, many want to be in the infrastructure of ministry with the senior leader but not all qualify. A gatekeeper is no ordinary person/member, but they should be trusted people. No leader should appoint anyone to oversee an area or areas of your ministry without them first being found faithful and committed to the vision and the senior leader. Oftentimes Pastors suffer great harm because they entrust and delegate their authority to people who don't qualify neither those who have not proven themselves to be worthy of keeping a gate in the ministry.

Pastors, if you have been having problems in the ministry and within areas in the ministry you may need to check the one that you have set in place as a gatekeeper. I will never forget when I was in the united states navy back in the late 1980s, I was chosen to be a Master at Arms inside of my command. My responsibility was to ensure that everything be kept intact in the absence of the company commander. He entrusted to me his full authority to operate in his stead and if anything went wrong during his absence, I would be the responsible party that would take the blame and receive the discipline. Therefore, I understood that I was supposed to adhere to the policies, rules and guidelines set forth by the company commander and hold those accountable that I was in charge over to do the same. Same way as a gatekeeper over an area of the ministry, your senior leader deputized you to keep order in your area by any means necessary. Let me give you a ministry example. I will never forget many years ago I was away on ministry assignment and I left one of my leaders in charge in my stead. I always make sure that the leaders that I leave in my place are fully capable and trained to address all matters and issues that may arise in a service. In my absence on this Sunday, there was a visiting lady who was possessed with a spirit that led her to want to be seen and make a big show before the congregation, I call it a "showmanship" spirit. Normally, our church service ends around 11 or so. However, on this Sunday, it was around 12:30pm and I had not heard from my staff regarding how the services went.

I arrived back in town around that same time, so I proceeded to the church find out what was going on and why had I not heard from anyone. Well, to my surprise I walked in and this woman had the microphone and she is "so called" prophesying to everyone in the church. Immediately when I walked in, I knew that this was not the spirit of God leading this woman. However, the person that I left in charge was standing by allowing this spirit to use this woman to take over the service. I immediately walked up and she became silent as I reached for the microphone to bring order and address this situation openly. The leader I left in my place did not adhere neither did he stick with the established protocol as he allowed things to get out of order. I said that for this purpose, as a gatekeeper over an area of ministry you are responsible for keeping that area of ministry in accordance to the protocol that has been established.

Just so that I am clear, I have no problem with prophetic gifts in operation because we are accustomed to apostolic and prophetic ministry in our church; but we believe that all things must be done in decency and in order as the Apostle Paul wrote to the churches. Therefore, I feel it needful to give some qualifications for the gatekeepers because not everyone qualifies or have what it takes to keep a gate/area of ministry.

1st qualification for a gatekeeper*- As a gatekeeper you must have the heart of the ministry 100%.* This means that you will do your all to protect the vision of the ministry and to give your all to see it become what God has ordained for it to be. If your heart is not all the way in the ministry then eventually it will become evident, because God will allow seasons and challenges to come your way to test your heart and sincerity to show you as well as your leader what's inside of you. Therefore, I've learned to embrace every challenge that I experience in ministry as it regards people. Sometimes things happen that appear bad but they turn out to be a blessing!! God allows things to happen to expose the hearts of people and to let the leaders know and see whose heart is truly 100% with the ministry.

In this hour Pastors, it's imperative for you to know that some who will say that they have the heart of the ministry up until they must be corrected, rebuked, sat down from leadership or when the senior leader decides or ministry move that they do not agree with. Most of the time when this happens, those who once said that they have the heart of the ministry you will find out that they didn't because adversity has a way of exposing the true heart and spirit of a person. Those who do not have the heart of the ministry are the ones who after being corrected or disciplined by the leader will no longer be found serving, giving, attending, doing or committing themselves to the work of ministry as they once did. They suddenly allow a “drawback” spirit to get on them and influence them to withdraw themselves from what they once did in the ministry. As a gatekeeper, you must learn to keep the heart of your church/ministry in the good times and during the challenging times. You must be able to take a licking and keep on ticking because as a gatekeeper everything done in your ministry/church is going to be to your liking, but you must maintain your heart for the ministry. Oftentimes, the devil as well as people will come to try and get your heart to turn from the ministry/church, but you must recognize his devices. The scripture declares in 2 Corinthians 2:11 “that we should not allow Satan to gain an advantage over us for we are not ignorant of his devices!” Gatekeepers keep your heart with all diligence.... You are responsible for keeping your heart and not allowing it to become defiled by the devil or people because Satan is masterful at sowing droplets into your heart to infect your it so he can ultimately cause you to abandon your gate, the ministry and your leader. I remember some time ago one of my key leaders who had been with me for a long time and served with me and under me in ministry fell prey to this very thing. Little did I know that this person was being influenced by Satan as the enemy was filling the heart of this person with all kinds of things that were infectious. They left the ministry, abandoned their place and position in the ministry because their heart became filled with satanic feelings.

When I refer to satanic feelings, I am referring to those feelings that Satan himself will try to strike up in people that serve around us that are laced with deception and lies. We must never forget that the scripture declares that Satan is the father of lies and he delights in leaders and gatekeepers who avail themselves to receive his lies...

(John 8:44). It is always Satan's objective to contaminate the hearts of those who serve in our ministries because he knows that the best way to hinder Apostolic churches/leaders is by attacking our help. One of the distinguishing qualities as to whether your church/ministry has an Apostolic mandate is or can be determined by how much Satan tries to attack your help! He will always attempt to stricken Apostles and Apostolic ministry by attacking and minimizing our help because Apostles are always thinking in terms of global expansion and enlargement.

Gatekeepers you cannot wear your feelings on your shoulders. As an Apostle, I'm hearing this terminology said quite a bit among people both within and outside the church called "I'm in my feelings." Sadly, there are too many saints now in the church that serve God and serve in the ministry/church per their feelings, thus when they feel like serving God or in the ministry they do, but then when they don't then they don't serve Him or in the ministry as they should. Many years ago, I can remember the commercial that's ensconced in my brain regarding the candy bars Almond Joy and Mounds. The slogan was "Sometimes I feel like a nut, sometimes I don't. Almond Joy has nuts, but Mounds don't..." I said that to say this; our feelings change from day to day, but we must learn how to be stable in our hearts regarding the ministry that God has called us to and the gate that your leader has put you over.

The Psalmist David said in Psalms 86:11, *Lord give me an undivided heart*.... This is what gatekeepers need in this hour so that they can endure in ministry for the long haul. Gatekeepers please understand that if you are easily offended then Satan is going to do everything he can to try and get your heart infected so he can ultimately get you to lose the heart of the ministry which will eventually cause you to become disinterested in manning the gate that your leader has given you authority to guard. In closing, I want to encourage all gatekeepers to keep your feelings in check as you labor to guard the gates of your ministry, undergird your leader and help to protect the peace and order in the house of God.

2nd qualification for a gatekeeper*- You must have and maintain the heart and spirit of your leader always*. In addition to having the heart of your ministry/church it's just as important as having and maintaining the heart and spirit of your leader at all times. There is nothing more important than the relationship between the gatekeeper and his/her senior leader. The devil will do anything that he can to affect this spiritual relationship because he doesn't want that spiritual connection to be intact. In this day and time, people allow some of the most trivial matters to cause them to be separated or disconnected from their leaders.

I want to take a moment to minster to someone that I believe is reading this book right now and you have allowed people, the devil and those who have left the ministry that you're under to influence you and speak into your ears about your spiritual leader. Please know that this is a plot of the devil to get you disconnected from your leader. There are many people sitting in churches and under leaders that they should not be under because they allowed seducing spirits that influenced people to cause you to be drawn away from where you have been called.

You know that you have been called to be a gatekeeper in your Pastor's ministry, but you allowed the devil or people to fill your heart with garbage and you left!

I want to speak into your life, whoever you may be that I am sensing in my spirit, it's time for you to pack up and return home to your spiritual father! You're likened unto the prodigal son who left his father's house prematurely and joined himself with the citizens of that country where he went and he found himself at his lowest of low, and the Bible says he then came to himself. In other words, he came to his senses and realized he needed to return home. I declare to those of you who tried to join yourself with another church and leader where you do not belong or fit, that it's time for you to return to your place of spiritual provision. Now that I've ministered to that person, let me return to talking about keeping the heart and spirit of your Pastor as a gatekeeper.

You cannot keep a gate in the ministry of your man of God's ministry if your heart can be so easily manipulated and turned against your leader. Some leaders fall victim to whisperers and busybodies that they allow to speak into their ears about their Pastors and they become contaminated with so much toxicity. You can never serve your senior leader when you're full of toxicity and the Lord won't allow you to pretend that you're with them and have their spirit when you don't. Gatekeepers you must not allow the "spirit of Ahithophel" to come upon and inundate you. You must be mindful of this spirit please!!! It's prevalent in the church today and spreading rapidly throughout the body of Christ!

In 1 Chronicles 27:33, tells of King David and Ahithophel his close counselor and companion. I classify Ahithophel as a gatekeeper on David's staff because he held a position in David's cabinet. He could also be likened to the relationship between a Pastor and an armor-bearer or assistant which I will speak on shortly. If there was anyone that knew personal things about the king it was

Ahithophel. Unfortunately, Ahithophel's heart was turned from David and he opened the gate for David's enemies to attack him and try to take the kingdom from him. (2 Samuel 16:20-21, 2 Samuel 17:1-4).

2 Samuel 16:20 Then said Absalom to Ahithophel, Give counsel among you what we shall do.
21 And Ahithophel said unto Absalom, Go in unto thy father's concubines, which he hath left to keep the house; and all Israel shall hear that thou art abhorred of thy father: then shall the hands of all that are with thee be strong.

2 Samuel 17:1 Moreover Ahithophel said unto Absalom, Let me now choose out twelve thousand men, and I will arise and pursue after David this night:
2 And I will come upon him while he is weary and weak handed, and will make him afraid: and all the people that are with him shall flee; and I will smite the king only:
3 And I will bring back all the people unto thee: the man whom thou seekest is as if all returned: so all the people shall be in peace.
4 And the saying pleased Absalom well, and all the elders of Israel.

Ahithophel, the gatekeeper's heart was turned against

his leader David and he opened the gate by giving David's son Absalom the information that he was privy to only because of his position as counselor to David. I mentioned the role of an Armor-bearer, but everyone may not have that title but as a gatekeeper you are permitted access to the Pastor just like the Armor-bearer. However, to those gatekeepers who serve in the role of armor-bearer allow me to admonish you on a few key points.

Some believe this role is not scriptural, but it is referenced many times. In 1 Samuel 14 Jonathan is speaking with his armor bearer regarding the Philistines. When Jonathan told his armor-bearer let's go over to the outpost he responded to Jonathan "Do all that you have in mind; go ahead; I am with you heart and soul." In other words, he was telling Jonathan *I've got your back.* Do you have the back of your Pastor and leader, or will you allow Satan to trick you and cause you to betray him or her?

Gatekeepers/ those who walk so closely with their senior leader, it's very important that you understand how to reverence the closeness between you and your leader and never allow yourself to become an agent of Satan and betray your leader.

Sadly, in the church, ministry and leadership betrayal is at an all-time high and rarely do you find loyal people in the ministry anymore. Some start off being loyal or should I say acting as if they are loyal to their leader, but they don't endure for the long haul. When I refer to leadership loyalty, I'm often reminded of the story of Elijah and Elisha. This is a perfect portrayal of loyalty found in the Bible. The word loyalty is defined as meaning a feeling of strong and unwavering support for someone or something. I believe in the story of Elijah and Elisha that Elisha demonstrated impeccable loyalty to his leader. Elisha knew what his leader Elijah had on him and he desired it to get on him! Everywhere Elijah went Elisha followed behind him no matter how much he tried to encourage him to stay behind. Elisha knew that his man of God had something on him that he desired, therefore he served him and remained loyal to him up until his man of God was taken up by God out of this earth. Because of his loyalty to his leader, Elisha received a double portion of his spirit upon his life and went forth to do great things in the kingdom.

Below are two key points to consider as you serve in close quarters of your leader:

1. **Know when to exit the room**

It is important to remember you are not your leader's peer. When you notice them gathering with their peers, unless you are instructed to remain simply excuse yourself. This protects your integrity from being tempted to share information you were not supposed to hear in the first place.

2. **Never expose your leader.**

When you are in proximity to your Pastor or leader you may learn or merely become privy to personal weaknesses, problems, or situations regarding their life. It is your responsibility to cover them in prayer and fasting with your lips closed to the people. The Bible speaks to this point with Noah and his two sons in Genesis 9:23.

And Noah began to be a farmer, and he planted a vineyard. Then he drank of the wine and was drunk, and became uncovered in his tent. And Ham, the father of Canaan, saw the nakedness of his father, and told his two brothers outside. But Shem and Japheth took a garment, laid it on both their shoulders, and went backward and covered the nakedness of their father. Their faces were turned away, and they did not see their father's nakedness. So Noah awoke from his wine, and knew what his younger son had done to him. Then he said: "Cursed be Canaan; a servant of servants he shall be to his brethren." And he said: "Blessed be the LORD, the God of Shem, and may

Canaan be his servant. May God enlarge Japheth, and may he dwell in the tents of Shem; and may Canaan be his servant."

I want to stop right here and take this opportunity to express my thankfulness to my spiritual sons and daughters who have remained loyal to my leadership over the many years. Through the storm and rains, ups and downs of ministry, although some did forsake me, however there are some who never disconnected or defected from their leader. Thanks to those who are a part of My Father's House Church and those of you who Pastor your own churches. As we can all agree, keeping the heart and spirit of your leader is essential and imperative as a gatekeeper. The devil knows what to use and who to use to sow seeds into your ears. I counsel you gatekeepers that your loyalty will be tested and tested greatly because many of you are privy to information and things concerning your leader that others are not. But, will you be the one to open the gate and give the devil access or not to come in?

Ahithophel did just that.... This hurt David tremendously and I want to say that in this day and time many of God's servants are hurting and struggling to trust the people again that they lead and are supposed to be gatekeepers because they've been burned and let down so many times in ministry. As I close this portion of talking about having your leaders' heart and spirit and keeping it, I can't help but think of the story of Joshua and Moses. The scripture rarely mentions Joshua during Moses administration other than he was Moses' minister in Exodus 24:13. However, Joshua was loyal to Moses until death. He kept the heart and spirit of his leader and walked right into his inheritance and became the next leader of Israel. He received this because he kept the heart and spirit of his leader!!

As I close, I want to emphasize the importance of what I'm saying regarding "maintaining the heart and spirit of your leader!" I am simply suggesting that it's easy to have your leaders' heart but can you keep/maintain it through it all?? After all, it was Peter who told Jesus *I will never deny you* but before the cock crowed, Peter had done so not one, twice but three times! I encourage every gatekeeper to ask God to help you to be fortified in your heart so that you will have and keep the heart of your leader for the long-haul. I pray you stand on guard at your gate as gatekeeper in the house of the Lord.

3rd qualification for a gatekeeper*- Gatekeepers must be faithful, committed and stable.* It's impossible for a gatekeeper to man his or her gate if they're not committed, faithful and stable. If you're not dependable, reliable and stable you are more of a hindrance than you are a helper to your senior leader! Unfortunately, in this day and time Pastors are have such a hard time with finding faithful, committed and stable people to man gates in the ministry. People are so "wishy washy," unstable in this hour and you cannot tell whether they will be with you in ministry the next week or not. Sadly, people vacillate from one extreme to another and unfortunately many areas of the ministry suffer, and gates go unmanned because of a lack of faithful, committed and stable people.

Many Pastors struggle to keep ministry afloat because every time you seemingly acquire a few new members, you appoint them to an area only to look around and find that they are no longer there. I've learned over my years of Apostolic leadership that everybody who comes into churches/ ministries are to be in a season of proving until their “newness” wears off. That’s when you begin to see and identify with the kind of people that you are working with. Everyone behaves “brand new” at first, but over a period they will inevitably resort back to their old self if they are not genuine!! Just give it some time as well as the individual. Do you remember when you first got your new car and you literally drove it carefully and were careful about how you took care of it? You wouldn’t allow anyone to eat or drink in it for fear of carpet or seats being stained etc. But after the newness wore off you found yourself eating and slacking in your care of that car because you didn’t value it as you once did when it was new.

The same ideology applies with some people in the ministry. They will value what they do, be faithful, committed and stable at first when things are new but gradually over a period, they suffer a fall off! It’s because their newness wore off! They were lavishing you with all kinds of impressive words, gifts, talents, that they were offering to the ministry but they lacked faithfulness, commitment and stability and now many of you Pastors have areas of ministry where there are no gatekeepers that are in place any longer because they were occupied by those whose newness wore off. I want to speak a word of encouragement to Pastors that you are never alone despite what people do or refuse to do or who comes and who goes. God is forever faithful!!!

When you have been called to do a work, you will have personnel problems from time to time but as I tell all my sons and daughters that sometimes you should have a downsizing plan in addition to your expansion plan!! There is a time and a season for everything! Ministry can be up and down sometimes especially when it concerns people. Until God sends in or others arise and become gatekeepers, just minimize the gates of your ministry.

Pastors maintain oversight of the house until your change comes and surely it will come quickly! God will send the people you need to get the job done and to man the gates! I want to prophesy to every pastor facing personnel problems... **Your help is on the way!!**

As for those of you who are not where you should be in your faithfulness, commitment and stability in the ministry it's time for you all to identify with those things that have prevented you from being that way and get on your gate and keep it with diligence. I want to prophesy to about 100 gatekeepers who are trying to work a gate, but you are carrying too much spiritual weight and baggage. It's your time to lay aside the weight so you can effectively man your gate in the ministry. Satan inspects the gates of every church and the people that man them he examines them to see where the weakest links are and who the weakest links are in the ministry. He will try and gain access into the ministry through your gate. Are you a weak

link??

CHAPTER 4
PRIMARY ROLES OF A GATEKEEPER

For a gatekeeper to secure their gate in the ministry they must understand their role. The definition of the word *role* is defined as a part that someone has in an activity or situation. Every gatekeeper has a role and primarily, it is to protect the Lord's house from all spiritual forces that seek to come in and/or arise within the community of the saints. The ministry/church should be a place of peace and unity not that of strife and confusion. Oftentimes leaders are not able to effectively do ministry and to fulfill its divine mandate because of the discord within the church/ministry among people. The Apostle

Paul said in the book of Ephesians 4: 3, "we must endeavor to keep the unity through the bond of peace." Therefore, gatekeepers are needed to oversee the gates of the ministry and to ensure that peace is sustained in the house of God. Below speaks on roles of the gatekeeper we will discuss the remainder of the chapter.

1st Role of a Gatekeeper*- Gatekeepers protect the Lords house-* The gatekeeper must not allow anything to enter through the gate that will hinder, hurt and bring catastrophic or collateral damage to the church/ministry or the leadership. Therefore, we must be watchful, spiritually discerning, and overly cautious because the enemy will at some point test your gate to see whether you are alert and on post. You are responsible for sounding the alarm loudly as soon as you see, hear or detect danger. Sadly, there is a diabolical mindset that is plaguing the body of Christ that is causing many saints to feel like they are wrong for exposing the work of evil that people do or seek to bring against the ministry/church. In this day and time gatekeepers, you cannot be loyal to personalities but to God and the one whom God has called to be your leader. Anyone regardless of who they are, gatekeepers should always be willing to sound the alarm and maintain allegiance to the vision of the house not people.

Cliques are so prevalent in the church. I can remember a time when the Lord led me to correct something that was discovered in the ministry. Amazingly, once I corrected and confronted the member, they abruptly left the ministry and some of their close friends and associates followed. This was because of people who were more loyal to friends, bosom buddies, partners in sin within the church rather than following their leader.

In the book of 1 Corinthians 1:12, the Apostle Paul began to address those in the church who were following certain people thus causing all kinds of strife, division, cliques and parties in the Corinthian church. Gatekeepers stay free from this at all cost. You're responsible for staying on the side of God and the established leadership of the house as they lead, according to the will of God.

I can remember years ago when a member advised me of something that could have been detrimental to the unity of the saints but the person that advised me asked to remain anonymous. I immediately begin to minister to this person that the church of the living God doesn't need confidential informants, but gatekeepers who have a heart for the ministry and leadership. The church needs people who do not mind confronting evil plots of the enemy that are meant to disrupt the unity of the house.

Therefore, as gatekeepers you must consider the following:

1. **You must be willing to confront and expose anything and anybody who poses a threat to the house of God or the leadership of the house regardless of who they are, what their status or position might be.**

Leadership loyalty over friendships is my motto in ministry. Everything has its place but kingdom business takes precedence over early and fleshly relationships, associations and affiliations.

2. **You are anointed to confront stuff at the gate and within the ministry.**

You don't have to become confrontational to confront things. There is a difference.

3. **You shouldn't concern yourselves with being confidential informants.**

As a gatekeeper, you are not there to win the opinion or to please men but to be pleasing to God and flow on one accord with Your leader.

Gatekeepers I want to stir up in you a boldness to hate evil and disorder in the house of God so much till you address every evil spirit that you see in operation and confront anyone who you see operating under the influence of a different spirit than what's in and on the house. It's time for spiritual warriors to arise up, man their gate and keep order in the Lord's house. You're anointed for this Gatekeeper. Protect the Lord's house and stay on your gate!

2nd role of the gatekeeper*- Keep the unity within the community of the saints-* Gatekeepers are to not allow anyone to come inside of the community of the saints to cause drama that could cause disunity within the community. You're responsible for addressing it at the gate or within the area of ministry that you oversee. As gatekeepers, you're responsible for holding all saints accountable for keeping the unity. You are the one that must extinguish fires that try to erupt in the ministry/church not add fuel to them. Whenever the enemy can keep the church/ministry at odds against one another then he can affect the momentum of the house of God. Remember in the Old Testament, there was confusion in the camp of Israel, and God had to cause Israel to stay at a place until the matters were dealt with. Any hint of confusion within the community should be quickly dealt with and settled. God caused Miriam to stay outside the camp because she and Aaron spoke against Moses's wife, an Ethiopian woman. This was significant enough to prove to us that God does not look favorably upon disunity, strife or discord in the house of God. The whole camp of Israel had to stand still until this matter was dealt with and those who were involved addressed. The Apostle Paul spoke about this in Galatians 5: 15 which reads:

> If you bite and devour one another, watch out or you will be destroyed by each other.

The devil would love for the church to self-destruct by fighting against one another. This is one of the major reasons why so many visions that God have given Pastors cannot be accomplished; because the people are not on one accord within the community of the Saints.

Gatekeepers your role is to work diligently to foster the spirit of unity in the house of God/ministry and help those who are at odds to settle their differences. We must usher the saints within the community who are fighting against one another to settle differences quickly and forgive one another for any wrongdoing that was committed.

Gatekeepers let us arise and secure our gates and refuse to allow anything and anybody to disrupt the work of ministry and the unity of the house of God. In the book of Romans 16, the Apostle Paul told us to *mark those who sows discord*. The word "mark" means to expose, to identify something or somebody! If we fail to mark those things and people that encourage disunity in the church/ministry, then that allows it to become contaminated causing the ministry to be adversely affected and segregated. Remember, *God is not the author of confusion, but of peace, as in all churches of the saints* (1 Corinthians 14:33).

3rd role of the gatekeeper- Help *to keep sheep within the gates*- This I believe is one of the most important roles of the gatekeeper. As you know the gate opens both ways and people can come into the ministry as well as leave. Gatekeepers are responsible for helping to keep God's people within the gates. Sadly, people come through the sheep gate of the church/ministry and leave out of the back gate of the church and seldom does anyone recognize their departure or go after them.

Speaking in terms of the back-gate, Pastors you must make sure that you appoint a gatekeeper on this gate that have a heart for people like you do because only those who do will feel compelled to go after sheep who leave out of the back gate. I sense that many Pastors commit themselves to much prayer, preparation and ministry of the word and then when they stand on the platform and look around the congregation many of those that they would normally see are not present at services. Every church/ministry should have what I call a "membership retention gate." This gate is manned by gatekeepers who are familiar with everyone who are a part of the church. Thus, when they observe some sheep are no longer attending the church as they once where they will move to reach out to them in hopes of reconciling them back into the church/ministry.

Gatekeepers, please understand that your Pastor shouldn't be the only one to pursue lost sheep that have strayed away from the fold. You should possess a passion to do this. As you follow closely and walk with your leader, their love and spirit for the sheep should become a part of you as well.

Furthermore, gatekeepers you are watchmen inside and outside the camp. Therefore, you should be able to see when someone within the flock could possibly be on the way leaving out of the ministry. A sign that a sheep is sickly to the shepherd is when the sheep lags away from the fold; they are less active as prior and their usual demeanor/activity changes. This is the same for the members. Those who were once faithful begin to drift. If your eyes are attentive to your gate you will see these changes long before your Pastor. You're responsible for encouraging that person to reconsider and help resolve issues that may exist. Gatekeepers you are responsible for helping the Pastor provide care for the flock, not allowing any sheep to leave out the gate through luring tactics of the enemy.

Gatekeepers are supposed to be there brothers and sisters' helpers. We are living in a day and time when people are leaving out of the church at an alarming rate and seemingly no one is concerned about it but the Pastor. Gatekeepers it's time for you to connect with your leaders' heart as it pertains to the sheep care and help them to keep the sheep inside the gate. I want to encourage every gatekeeper to look within the house and see the sheep that have left out of the gate without anyone going after or checking on them and go and attempt to reconcile your brother and sister back into the community of the saints. Help your Pastor or senior leader to keep the flock of God intact because you are anointed to keep the gates of the ministry.

If you are a gatekeeper, it's time for you to get on your gate!!! Intercessors get on your gate!! Youth ministers get on your gate!!! Whatever your gate in this hour get on it and do it to the best of your ability.

CHAPTER 5
WHEN THE GATEKEEPERS BECOME DISTRACTED- "GATE KEEPERS GONE BAD"

As I prepare to conclude the writing of this book, I need to release this to leaders both the senior leadership and their subordinates. There are times when gatekeepers become distracted and they allow themselves to become a hindrance to the momentum of the ministry while serving as a gatekeeper in the church/ministry. I'm reminded of how years ago those who were supposed to be gatekeepers in ministry with me allowed themselves to become distracted by works of the flesh and sinful activity. Unfortunately, when gatekeepers become distracted, they become the bait at the gate for Satan. He will have unlimited access in and out of the ministry because the gatekeeper has become distracted. Pastors and senior leaders never be intimidated or afraid to remove gatekeepers off the gate. Pastors reestablish order at the gates. This entails removing key people sometimes in the ministry, you must do what needs to be done to safeguard the favor, blessing and unity within the community of the saints.

Pastors be bold in this hour and keep the house of God and let us prepare God's bride for his return. Gatekeepers keep your focus and stay watchful and vigilant for our adversary the devil is walking about like a roaring lion seeking whom he may devour.

APOSTLE'S FINAL THOUGHTS

It is my sincere prayer that every Apostle, Bishop, Pastor and senior leader along with those who serve with and under them in ministry will get this book and study it together as a group. We must have a corporate strategy implemented within the churches/ministries among the gatekeepers so that everyone will know what to look for and how to combat issues that arise within the gates and how to confront anything and anybody that attempts to gain access through the gates. I encourage all leaders to have periodic gatekeepers pass down meetings. This will facilitate the environment where all gatekeepers will be in the loop regarding those things that the enemy is trying to do and bring against the ministry and to devise a strategy for us to combat them. I've concluded that most successful companies have periodic weekly extensive board and staff meetings to discuss the company however in some churches/ministries the staff rarely have meetings, trainings etc. We must incorporate this into our weekly agendas, because from day to day the enemy never ceases his assault against our churches/ministries. I've taken the liberty to include note pages to notate specific nuggets that will become action items for your ministry or church. I encourage all gatekeepers to be sober minded and vigilant in this hour and let us man our gates until the Lord returns!

APOSTLE XAVIER D. MADISON, SR.

APOSTLE/ MY FATHER'S HOUSE CHURCH
VOICES OF TRUTH INTERNATIONAL MINISTERIAL ALLIANCE, INTERNATIONAL PRESIDING PRELATE

THE AUTHOR

Apostle Xavier D. Madison, Sr. Is a native of Mobile, Alabama who relocated to Baton Rouge, Louisiana at five years old. After being honorably discharged from the United States Navy, he worked in the chemical industry for many years. Apostle Madison served faithfully in various leadership capacities such as men's ministry leader, cell group leader, youth ministry leader, overseer of Christian education, greeting ministry overseer, and as a faithful servant/assistant to his Pastor prior to the birthing of My Father's House Church.

Under his leadership, My Father's House Church has become a thriving, vibrant, inner-city community-based church with a global reach. Apostle Madison has birthed many sons and daughters in ministry and provides spiritual covering for them as they pastor their own churches and continues to provide leadership, support, wisdom and spiritual guidance to those who remain connected to him. Apostle attended International Fellowship of Faith Churches Bible Institute and attended seminary where he earned a degree in Theology in 2008. In 2010, he was officially consecrated as Bishop and was inducted into the College of Bishops. God begin to deal with him regarding the Apostolic call that was upon his life, and in 2011 the Apostolic mantle was released upon him. Shortly after embracing the Apostolic call, he began to give birth to vision that God has put in his heart, by organizing an international alliance named Voices of Truth International Ministerial Alliance (VOTIMA).

This alliance consists of five-fold ministry gifts that have covenanted together to re-establish kingdom order in the earth. The alliance also serves to equip pastors and churches with the tools to be effective in their ministry endeavors. He has hosted "Throne Room Broadcast" and "Voice of Truth" television broadcasts for over ten years. He is married to Lady Schantia Madison, and they have four wonderful children. The Madison's are successful entrepreneurs and reside in Louisiana.

NOTES

NOTES

NOTES